Basics

flattened crimp
1 Hold the crimp bead using the tip of your chainnose pliers. Squeeze the pliers firmly to flatten the crimp. Tug the clasp to make sure the crimp has a solid grip on the wire. If the wire slides, remove the crimp bead and repeat the steps with a new crimp bead.
2 Test that the flattened crimp is secure.

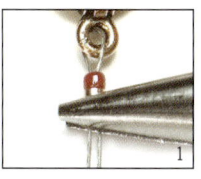 

folded crimp
1 Position the crimp bead in the notch closest to the crimping pliers' handle.
2 Separate the wires and firmly squeeze the crimp.

3 Move the crimp into the notch at the pliers' tip and hold the crimp as shown. Squeeze the crimp bead, folding it in half at the indentation.
4 Test that the folded crimp is secure.

half-hitch knot
Bring the thread out of a bead and form a loop perpendicular to the thread between beads. Bring the needle under the thread away from the loop. Then go back over the thread and through the loop. Pull gently so the knot doesn't tighten prematurely.

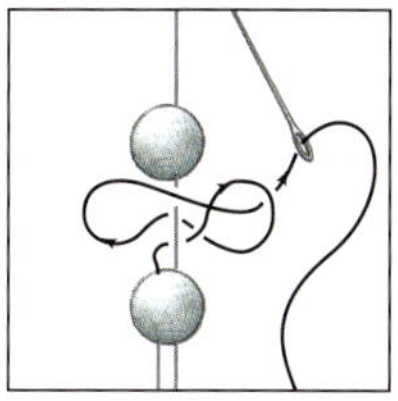

opening and closing loops and rings
1 Hold the loop or jump ring with two pairs of chainnose pliers or chainnose and roundnose pliers, as shown.
2 To open the loop or jump ring, bring one pair of pliers toward you and push the other pair away.
3 While the loop or jump ring is open, string on beads, chain, or other elements. Reverse the steps to close the opened loop or ring.

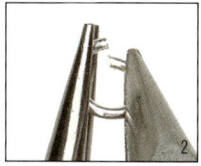 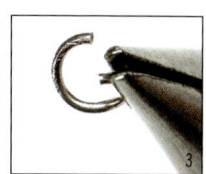

plain loops
1 Trim the head pin or wire to ⅜ in. (1cm) above the top bead. Make a right-angle bend in the wire close to the bead.
2 Grab the wire's tip with roundnose pliers. Roll the wire to form a half circle. Release the wire.

3 Reposition the pliers in the loop and continue rolling.
4 The finished loop should form a circle centered above the bead.

wrapped loops
1 Make sure you have at least 1¼ in. (3.2cm) of wire above the bead. With the tip of your chainnose pliers, grasp the wire directly above the bead. Bend the wire (above the pliers) into a right angle.
2 Using roundnose pliers, position the jaws in the bend.

3 Bring the wire over the top jaw of the roundnose pliers.
4 Keep the jaws vertical and reposition the pliers' lower jaw snugly into the loop. Curve the wire downward around the bottom of the roundnose pliers. This is the first half of a wrapped loop.

5 Position the chainnose pliers' jaws across the loop.
6 Wrap the wire around the wire stem, covering the stem between the loop and the top of the bead. Trim the excess wire and press the cut end close to the wraps with chainnose pliers.

Bead & Button • Easy Beaded Necklaces

Shimmering shell set

Chances are you won't find a shell this magical lying on a nearby beach. But since you can buy one, add a little of your own magic by putting it together with some crystal bicones and simulated opals for a beautiful necklace and earring set.

necklace

1 This necklace is 18 in. (46cm) long without the clasp. Begin by cutting a 20-in. (50cm) length of flexible beading wire. Slide the shell to the center. The organic shape requires some balancing to make it hang properly. To stabilize the shell, string an 11º and a 6mm simulated opal on each side of the focal bead (**photo a**).

2 String a small spacer, a green bicone, a large spacer, a 10mm amethyst, a large spacer, and a green bicone. This pattern will not repeat.

3 String a small spacer, an 8mm opal, and a small spacer. This is group one.

4 Group two is strung as follows: green bicone, green 15º, purple bicone, green 15º, opal briolette, green 15º, purple bicone, green 15º, green bicone (**photo b**).

5 Alternate groups one and two until you've strung a total of six 8mm opals and six briolettes.

6 String a small spacer, a 6mm opal, a small spacer, and a green bicone.

7 String an 11º, a crimp bead, and an 11º.

8 Go through one end of the clasp and back through the two seeds and the crimp bead. Pull the tail tight and crimp (see "Basics," p. 3 and **photo c**).

9 Repeat steps 2–8 to finish the other side. Trim the tails.

earrings

1 Cut a 4-in. (10cm) length of 24-gauge half-hard sterling silver wire.

2 Start a wrapped loop (see "Basics") at one end of the wire and string a

a

c

b

d

e

f

tip
color wheel

Use a color wheel, like the simple one shown here, if you want help choosing colors for your beading projects. More complex color wheels can be found at art supply and craft stores as well as various Web sites. Besides the basic primary (red, blue, and yellow) and secondary (violet, green, and orange) colors shown here, some wheels show a full range of tints, shades, and hues. These can be helpful for choosing complementary (colors opposite each other) as well as analogous (colors adjacent to each other) color schemes.

briolette (**photo d**) before finishing the wrap (**photo e**).

❸ On the other end, string a purple bicone, a small spacer, a green bicone, a large spacer, a 10mm amethyst, a large spacer, a green bicone, a small spacer, and a purple bicone (**photo f**). Make a small wrapped loop above the purple bicone.

❹ Open the bottom loop of the earring finding (see "Basics"), attach the beaded component, and close the loop.

❺ Make a second earring to match the first. ⊙ – *Debbie Nishihara*

Contact Debbie at dnishihara@beadandbutton.com.

materials

18-in. (46cm) necklace
- shell bead (Eclectica, 262-641-0910)
- simulated opal beads:
  12 10mm briolettes
  12 8mm rondelles
  4 6mm rondelles
- **2** 10mm faceted amethyst rondelles
- crystal bicones:
  30 5mm, green
  24 4mm, purple
- seed beads:
  6 size 11º, purple
  50 size 15º, green
- **4** 11mm silver spacers
- **30** 4mm silver spacers
- flexible beading wire, size .014
- toggle clasp (this one from Green Girl Studios, www.greengirlstudios.com)
- **2** crimp beads

earrings
- **2** 10mm simulated opal briolettes
- **2** 10mm faceted amethyst rondelles
- crystal bicones:
  4 5mm, green
  4 4mm, purple
- **4** 11mm silver spacers
- **4** 4mm silver spacers
- 8 in. (20cm) 24-gauge sterling silver wire
- **2** earring wires

Tools: roundnose, chainnose, and crimping pliers, diagonal wire cutters

Leafy fringe necklace

Make a simple seed bead necklace more interesting by embellishing it with a fringe of multicolored glass leaf beads.

necklace base

❶ Center 36 size 8º seed beads on 2 ft. (61cm) of flexible beading wire. Tape one end.
❷ String a leaf, pointed end first, then six 8ºs (**photo a**).
❸ String a leaf, an 8º, a leaf, and six 8ºs, pointing the leaves toward each other (**photo b**).
❹ Repeat step 3 twice, alternating the leaf colors (**photo c**).
❺ String a crimp bead and the clasp, then go back through the crimp and the next few 8ºs.
❻ Crimp the crimp bead (see "Basics," p. 3 and **photo d**) and then trim the excess wire.
❼ Repeat steps 2–6 on the other end.

fringed center

❶ Thread a needle with 1 yd. (.9m) of Fireline. Tie the line to the base necklace with a half-hitch knot (see "Basics"), placing the knot two beads from the center. Go through two beads toward the center and make another knot.
❷ Refer to the fringe illustration on page 7. Pick up 36 Charlottes, a leaf, and another Charlotte. Turn, skip the last bead, and go back through the leaf and six beads (**figure, a–b**).
❸ Pick up 12 Charlottes. Turn, skip the last bead, and go back through the next five beads (**figure, b–c**).
❹ Pick up three Charlottes. Turn, skip the last bead, and go back through the next two beads. Continue through the next six beads toward the stem, then go up through six more beads (**figure, c–d** and **photo e**).
❺ Pick up three Charlottes, a leaf, and a Charlotte. Turn, skip the last bead, and

a

b

c

f

i

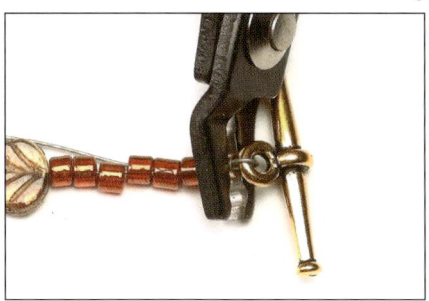
d

g

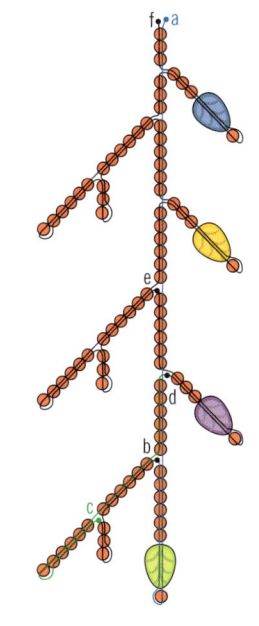

e

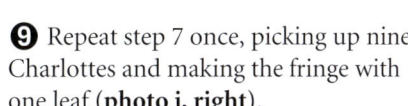
h

materials

16-in. (41cm) necklace
- 34 Czech pressed glass leaves in four related colors
- 10g size 8º Japanese seed beads
- 5g size 13º Charlottes
- 2 yd. (1.8cm) Fireline fishing line, 6 lb. test
- 2 ft. (60cm) flexible beading wire, .014
- toggle clasp
- 2 crimp beads
- beading needles, #12

Tools: diagonal wire cutters, crimping pliers

go back through the leaf and three beads. Go up through the next six beads (**figure, d-e** and **photo f**).

6 Repeat steps 3–5 twice. Go through the last three Charlottes to finish the fringe (**figure, e-f** and **photo g**).

7 Go through four 8ºs, then make a half-hitch knot. Pick up 24 Charlottes and make the next fringe with three leaves (**photo h**).

8 Repeat step 7 twice, picking up 18 Charlottes and making the fringe with two leaves (**photo i, left**).

9 Repeat step 7 once, picking up nine Charlottes and making the fringe with one leaf (**photo i, right**).

10 When you've made the last fringe on the end, tie a half-hitch knot, go through an 8º, then tie another knot. Sew through a few more beads. Dot the knots with glue, let dry, and trim the Fireline.

11 Start another yard of Fireline at the center of the necklace and repeat steps 1–10 to add fringe to the other side. ○
– Lea Rose Nowicki

Contact Lea at 3700 S. 61st St. #14, Milwaukee, WI 53220, (414) 329-2796.

tip

faster fringing

Making fringe is the most time-consuming part of this project, so change the bead count, increase the bead size, or simplify the design to fit your schedule.

Cotillion choker

Step back in time and recall the grace and elegance of a bygone era. Create a necklace that is as stylish today as it was at its debut.

necklace

1 Measure your neck to determine the finished length of the necklace, subtract 1 in. (2.5cm) for the clasp, and cut two pieces of chain to this length.
2 Cut a 3-in. (7.6cm) piece of wire. Start a wrapped loop (see "Basics," p. 3) at one end. Slide the loop into one of the two long links at the center of one chain. Finish the wraps (**photo a**).
3 String a seed bead, a teardrop (tapered end first), and a seed bead on the wire. Start a wrapped loop in the same plane as the first. Slide the loop into a long link on the second chain as before (**photo b**). Make sure there are no twists in the chain and that the component lays flat. Finish the wraps (**photo c**).
4 Repeat steps 2–3 three times, working toward one end of the chains. Connect each new wrapped loop in the next long link. Be sure to orient each teardrop in the same direction as the others.
5 Attach four more components as above, working from the center to the opposite end.

dangles

1 String a seed bead, a teardrop (wide end first), and a seed bead on a head pin.
2 String a 4mm fire-polished bead and a seed bead three times (**photo d**).
3 Start a wrapped loop. Slide it into one of the center links on the lower chain (**photo e**). Finish the wraps.
4 Repeat steps 1–3 three more times. As you work along the chain toward one end, use one fewer 4mm bead and seed bead for each successive dangle (**photo f**).
5 Repeat steps 1–4 to attach four additional dangles, working from the center toward the opposite end.

materials

16-in. (41cm) necklace
- **18** 6 x 5mm fire-polished teardrop beads
- **12** 4mm fire-polished round beads
- 1g size 11º seed beads
- 1 yd. (.9m) triple long-and-short chain (Rio Grande, www.riogrande.com)
- 24 in. (61cm) 24-gauge wire
- **10** 3-in. (7.6cm) head pins
- **2** 4mm jump rings
- S-hook clasp

Tools: chainnose and roundnose pliers, diagonal wire cutters

a

b

e

g

h

c

f

d

finishing

❶ String a seed, a teardrop (wide end first), and a seed bead on a head pin and start a wrapped loop. To make a swag in the chain, slide the loop into a long link on the upper chain 1 in. from the last component. On the lower chain, slide the loop into a long link about 1½ in. (3cm) from the last component (**photo g**). Finish the wraps. Repeat on the other end of the necklace.

❷ Cut off the remaining lower chain. Open a pair of jump rings (see "Basics") and connect one to each end of the chain. Close the rings.

tip

vintage vogue

To add a more authentic quality to this necklace, consider using vintage beads. For online bead sources, check our links at www.beadandbutton.com/bnb/community/links/.

clasp

Slide one end of the S-hook clasp into one of the jump rings and lightly compress that end with chainnose pliers so it won't fall off (**photo h**). ○

– Terri Torbeck

Contact Terri in care of Kalmbach Publishing at books@kalmbach.com.

a

b

c

Gemstone wrap

Emphasize your favorite gemstone by using an interesting assortment of beads in different shapes and sizes. These directions are for an eight-strand necklace, but that number can easily be adjusted to suit your assortment of beads.

❶ Determine the finished length of your necklace, subtract the clasp length, and add 5 in. (13cm). Cut eight strands of flexible beading wire to that length.

❷ Tape one end of each wire to prevent the beads from sliding off and string gemstones onto each. Space the larger stones with seed beads, if desired (**photo a**). You can also incorporate strands of seed beads with your stones to add fullness and sparkle.

❸ Separate the strands into pairs. Working with one pair of beading wires at a time, string a crimp bead and a silver spacer over both wires. Go through the loop end of the clasp and back through the spacer and crimp (**photo b**). Tighten the wires until they form a small loop around the clasp and crimp the crimp bead (see "Basics," p. 3). Take the wire tails through a bead or two before trimming them. Repeat with the remaining pairs of wire.

❹ A toggle needs an extender so it can pivot enough to fit through the clasp loop. If your toggle already has an extender, repeat step 3 to crimp the wires to it. If not, create an extender as follows: Attach a split ring to the toggle's loop and to the end link of a 1-in. (2.5cm) piece of chain. Position the toggle so the bar is parallel to the chain (**photo c**). Unless you want the extra length, cut off any links that extend beyond the bar. If the chain links are too small to hold four pairs of beading wires, attach a split ring to the end link.

❺ Snug up the beads so no wire shows. Attach the beading wires to the toggle extender as in step 3. Give the necklace a slight twist or two when you wear it. ●
– Mindy Brooks

Contact Mindy, editor of Bead&Button *magazine, at editor@beadandbutton.com.*

materials

- 36-in. (.9m) strand small gemstone chips
- 3 16-in. strands irregularly shaped gemstones
- 5 16-in. (41cm) strands 2mm round gemstones
- 10g or more size 11º or 12º seed beads to match gemstones
- 8 2.5mm silver spacer beads
- toggle clasp (this one from Scottsdale Bead Supply, www.scottsdalebeadsupply.com)
- 2 split rings
- flexible beading wire, .010
- 8 crimp beads

Tools: crimping pliers, diagonal wire cutters
Optional: 1-in. (2.5cm) piece of chain

Tiered drops

Queen Elizabeth inspired this choker. No, it wasn't the monarch herself, but a necklace worn by actress Cate Blanchett in the historical film *Elizabeth*. While Blanchett's jewelry incorporated intricate metalsmithing, this choker requires uncomplicated wirework. Simple wraps secure dangling pearls and crystals. The project is quick and easy, perfect for the beginner beader or anyone desiring an elegant necklace. These directions are for the necklace pictured above right. At left is one of many possible variations.

dangles

❶ On a head pin, string a pearl and a 4mm bicone crystal, then make a wrapped loop (see "Basics," p. 3, and **photo a**, p. 12). Make 16 more dangles like this one and set aside.
❷ String two pearls on a head pin and make a wrapped loop (**photo b**, p. 12). Make 15 more pearl components like this one.
❸ String a 6mm bicone crystal and a 4mm bicone on a head pin. Start a wrapped loop, slide a pearl component into the loop (**photo c**, p. 12), then finish the wraps. Make five more dangles like this one.
❹ Repeat step 3 using a 6mm round crystal instead of a 6mm bicone (**photo d**, p. 12). Make five more dangles.

necklace base

❶ Using 2 ft. (61cm) of 24-gauge wire, make a wrapped loop at one end.
❷ String a pearl, the loop on one of the short dangles from step 1 of "dangles," and a pearl (**photo e**, p. 12).
❸ Slide a 6mm round crystal dangle from step 4 of "dangles" next to the last

pearl. Wrap the wire around the dangle between the two pearls (**photo f**, p. 12).
❹ Repeat step 2.
❺ Repeat step 3 using a 6mm bicone crystal dangle (**photo g**).
❻ Repeat steps 2–5 seven times.
❼ Make a wrapped loop at the other end of the wire.

adjustable chain closure
❶ Open a jump ring (see "Basics") and attach it to a wrapped loop at the end of the wire and 1 in. (2.5cm) of chain (**photo h**). Close the ring.
❷ Open a jump ring and use it to attach the clasp to the other end of the chain. Close the ring.
❸ Repeat step 1 at the other end of the necklace, using 3 in. (7.6cm) of chain.
❹ String a pearl and a 4mm bicone crystal on a head pin and make a wrapped loop. Make a second dangle.
❺ Use a jump ring to attach the two dangles to the chain (**photo i**). ○
– Annie Conkill

Contact Annie at andraneal@verizon.net.

materials
12½–15-in. (32–38cm) choker
- **90** 6mm round pearls
- Swarovski crystals:
  33 4mm bicones
  8 6mm bicones
  8 6mm rounds
- **54** head pins, fine
- **4** in. (10cm) chain with 4mm links
- **4** 4mm jump rings
- lobster claw clasp
- **2** ft. (61cm) 24-gauge wire

Tools: roundnose and chainnose pliers, diagonal wire cutters

a

e

b

f

c

g

d

h

i

Easy suede necklace

Dangle a few chunky gemstones from suede lacing for a fast and easy-to-make necklace. Choose colors that go with your wardrobe or adapt the design to beads you have on hand.

The tan necklace, above left, has large dangles made with nuggets and spacers strung on head pins. On the violet necklace, above right, each large dangle is embellished with a smaller one, which can be a charm or a small bead on a head pin.

❶ String a nugget with or without spacers on each eye pin (if you plan to add small dangles) or 2-in. (5cm) head pin. Make a plain loop (see "Basics," p. 3 and **photo a**) above the end bead.

❷ To make small dangles that hang below the large ones, string a 6mm bead on each 1-in. (2.5cm) head pin. Make a plain loop above each bead (**photo b**).
❸ To attach the small dangles to the nuggets, open one loop on each eye pin (see "Basics"), slide on a small dangle (**photo c**, p. 14), and close the loops.
❹ Cut one 16-in. (41cm) and two 6-in. (15cm) lengths of suede.
❺ Slide a crimp end onto one of the suede ends. Squeeze the crimp end with chainnose pliers until it closes tightly around the lacing (**photo d**, p. 14). Attach crimp ends to each of the remaining suede ends.
❻ Open the loop above each nugget and attach the nuggets to the crimp ends on the short pieces of suede

a

b

(**photo e**, p. 14). Close the loops.

❼ Place the long suede piece horizontally across your work surface. Hold the two shorter pieces together and fold them in half. Attach them to the center of the long suede piece with a lark's head knot (see "lark's head knot," below, and **photo f**).

❽ Open a jump ring (see "Basics") or split ring and attach it to the crimp end on one end of the long suede piece. Attach a spring ring or lobster claw clasp to the crimp end on the other end (**photo g**). ● – *Lynne Dixon-Speller*

Contact Lynne in care of Kalmbach Publishing at books@kalmbach.com.

c

d

e

f

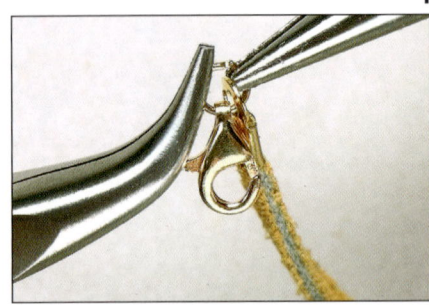
g

materials

- **4** 25mm gemstone nuggets
- **4** 2-in. (5cm) eye pins (for dangles) or head pins
- **4** 1-in. (2.5cm) head pins (for small bead dangles)
- **3** ft. (.9m) suede lacing
- **6** end crimps for cord (Rio Grande, www.riograde.com)
- 6mm jump ring or split ring
- spring ring or lobster claw clasp

Tools: roundnose and chainnose pliers, diagonal wire cutters

Optional: 4 6mm beads or small charms for dangles, **8** 6mm flat spacers

lark's head knot

1 Fold a cord in half and lay it behind the cord with the fold pointing up.
2 Bring the fold around the cord from back to front. Pull the ends through the fold and tighten.

1

2

Cross-woven bail

If you are puzzled about stringing a top-drilled pendant, try this simple variation on cross-needle weave. Let the pendant's colors guide your choice of crystals, gemstones, and seed beads, and enjoy the easy sophistication of the finished piece.

❶ Cut two 1½ yd. (1.4m) strands of beading wire. String enough seed beads to the center of the two strands to make a bail around the pendant. String the pendant over the seed beads (**photo a**).

❷ String a seed bead, a 6mm stone, and a seed bead over all four strands. Split the four strands into two pairs (**photo b**).

❸ On one pair of wires, string a seed bead, a 4mm stone, a seed bead, a 4mm stone, and a seed bead.

a

b

Repeat on the other pair of wires.

❹ Cross the pairs through a 6mm stone (**photo c**).

❺ On the first pair, string one seed bead, then split the pair apart. On one strand, alternate a seed bead and a 4mm stone four times and end with a seed bead. Repeat on the second strand. Then string a seed bead, a 6mm stone, and a seed bead over both strands (**photo d**).

❻ Split the first pair of strands apart again. On the first strand, string a seed bead, a main color crystal, a seed bead, an accent color crystal, a seed bead, a main color crystal, and a seed bead. Then alternate a 4mm stone and a seed bead three times and end with a 4mm stone (**photo e**). Repeat the sequence four times or to the desired length, ending with the seed bead and crystal section. Repeat for the second strand. Add five seed beads to the end of the second strand so it hangs slightly lower.

❼ String a seed bead, a crimp bead, and half the clasp over both strands. Go back through the crimp with both strands, adjust the tension, and crimp the crimp bead (see "Basics," p. 3). Trim the tails (**photo f**).

❽ Repeat steps 5–7 to finish the other side of the necklace. ○ – *Anna Nehs*

Anna is an assistant editor at Bead&Button. Contact her at beadbiz@hotmail.com or visit her website, beadivine.biz.

c

e

d

f

materials

17-in. (43cm) necklace
- 2-in. (5cm) pendant with a top-drilled hole
- gemstone beads:
  84 4mm round
  4 6mm round
- 4mm bicone crystals:
  40 main color
  20 accent color
- size 11º or 15º Japanese seed beads
- flexible beading wire, size .010
- **2** crimp beads
- clasp

Tools: crimping pliers, wire cutters

Lacy seed bead necklace

Make this lacy necklace by weaving together inexpensive seed beads. The pattern is easy to work and lends itself to many variations. You can use different size beads or add drops or additional loops to the bottom (see the green necklace on p. 17 or the pink one above). You might also make the connector bead and the beads that link the various loops a different color, size, or shape. Crystals or pressed glass beads make especially pretty connector beads. Another option is to flip the design and add the same three-loop motif above the connector bead as well as below it (see the black and silver necklace above and **figure 7**). As in tatting, which inspired this stitch, the lace is formed by connecting loops together.

❶ Thread a needle with 1–2 yd. (.9–1.8m) of conditioned Nymo. Pick up six MC beads, sew through the clasp loop, and pick up two more MC beads, leaving a 4–6-in. (10–15cm) tail to weave in later. Go through all eight beads again and continue through the first three beads a third time (**figure 1**).
❷ Pick up 13 MC beads and go through the last two that you exited on

materials

- size 11º seed beads:
  8g main color (MC)
  3g accent color (AC)
- clasp
- Nymo D beading thread
- beeswax or Thread Heaven for conditioning Nymo
- beading needles, #12 or 13

tip

conditioning thread

Before you thread your needle, pull Nymo through beeswax or Thread Heaven to help prevent tangling and fraying. Maintaining tension as you do so will help release any excess stretch.

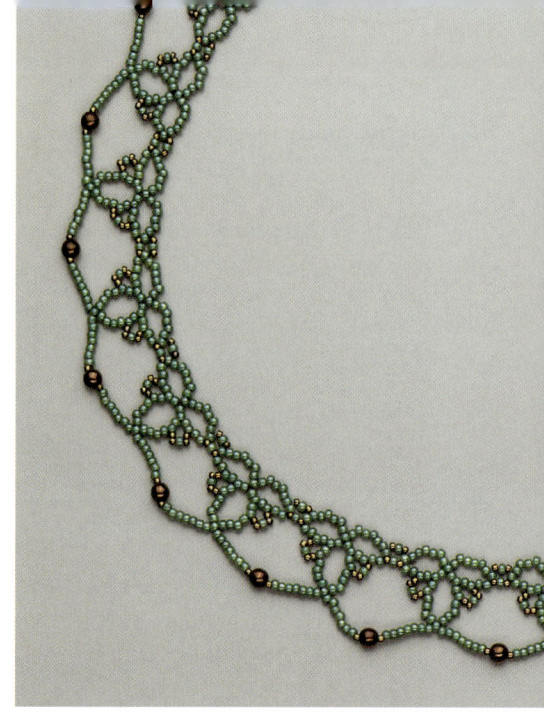

the previous loop and the first seven of the new loop (**figure 2**).

❸ Pick up 14 MC beads and go through the last bead you exited on the previous loop (**figure 3**). This is the connector bead.

❹ Continue through two beads in the first large loop (**figure 4, a–b**). Pick up ten MC beads and go through the corresponding two beads on the second large loop (**figure 4, b–c**). Cross over to the first large loop and go through the same two beads that you went through at the beginning of this step and the next two beads (**figure 4, c–d**).

❺ Here's where the pattern gets interesting because you can start playing with color. Pick up two MC beads, one AC bead, and two MC beads. Go through two beads of the ten-bead loop toward the connector bead (**figure 5, a–b**). Continue through the same two beads of the first large loop and four beads of the second large loop (**figure 5, b–c**). String two MC, one AC, and two MC and go through the last two beads of the ten-bead loop (**figure 5, c–d**). Continue through the first two beads of the second large loop, the connector bead and eight beads along the top of the second large loop (**figure 5, d–e**).

❻ String an AC, an MC, an AC, two MC, an AC, an MC, and an AC and go through the last two beads you exited on the second large loop. Continue through the first five beads added in this step (**figure 6**).

❼ Repeat steps 3–7 for the desired length. Stop just before repeating step 7 for the last time.

❽ When the necklace is long enough, repeat step 7, stringing only MC beads and catching the other clasp part in this final ring of beads. Make sure the beadwork is not twisted. Go through the loop once or twice more to reinforce it,

and tie two or three half-hitch knots (see "Basics," p. 3) between beads. Go through a few beads before cutting the thread.

❿ Knot off the starting tail in its loop as in step 9. ● – *Lynda Roubineau*

You can see Lynda's work at www.thebeadgoddess.com. Contact her by phone at (916) 214-3919 or by e-mail at lr@thebeadgoddess.com.

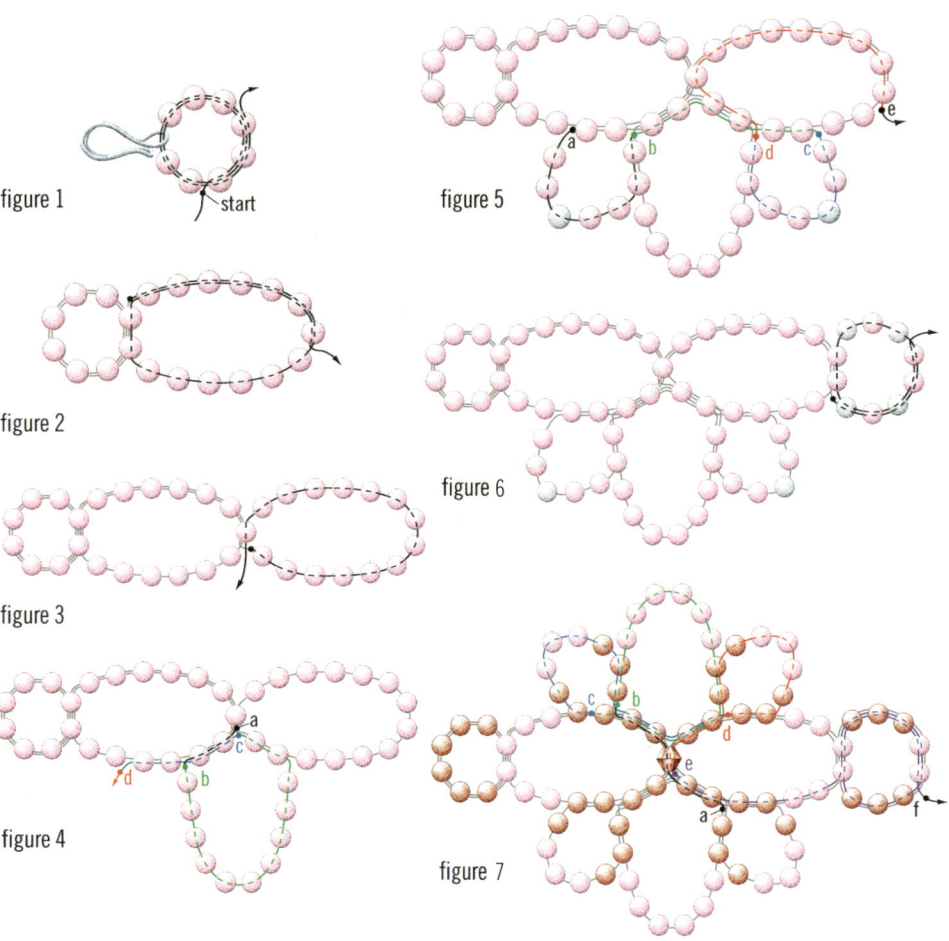

Bead&Button • Easy Beaded Necklaces

Charmed necklace

Combine seashell-shaped beads with pearls and coral to make this delightful necklace version of the classic charm bracelet. For simplicity, make the dangles first, then assemble the necklace.

make the cone-shaped shell dangles

❶ Cut four five-link pieces of chain (**photo a**).
❷ String one or two branch coral beads on a head pin and make the first half of a wrapped loop (see "Basics," p. 3). Make a total of 44 coral dangles.
❸ Attach the loop on one coral dangle to the end link on one five-link piece of chain and finish the wraps (**photo b**). This is the bottom link of one coral-embellished chain.
❹ Add ten more coral dangles to the five-link chain as follows: two more to the bottom link (a total of three dangles) and two dangles to each of the four remaining links.
❺ Repeat steps 3–4 using the other three chain pieces.
❻ Cut a 4-in. (10cm) length of 24-gauge wire. Make the first half of a wrapped loop at one end, attach it to the top link of one of the embellished chains (**photo c**), and finish the wraps.
❼ String a cone-shaped shell onto the wire, wide end first (**photo d**). Start a wrapped loop above the cone and set it aside (**photo e**).
❽ Repeat steps 6–7 with the three remaining five-link chains and cone-shaped shells.

make the other shell dangles

❶ String a pearl on a head pin and make a wrapped loop above the pearl (**photo f**). Trim the wire tail. Make a total of nine pearl dangles.
❷ Cut a 4-in. length of wire. Start a wrapped loop and link it to the loop on one pearl dangle (**photo g**). Finish the wraps.
❸ String an 18mm shell bead on the wire (**photo h**). Start a wrapped loop and set the piece aside.
❹ Repeat steps 2–3 with the remaining 10 and 18mm shells. For the large center shell, connect three pearl dangles to the bottom wrapped loop (see **photo i**).

assemble the necklace

❶ Fold the remaining long piece of chain (approximately 22 in./56cm) in half to find the center link. Connect the large shell dangle to the center link and finish the wraps (**photo i**).
❷ Skip three links to the right of the center link and attach a cone-shaped dangle to the fourth link (**photo j**). Finish the wraps.